Learn to Move!

I DO CHEERLEADING!

By Bray Jacobson

Gareth Stevens Publishing

Please visit our website, www.garethstevens.com. For a free color catalog of all our high-quality books call toll free 1-800-542-2595 or fax 1-877-542-2596.

Library of Congress Cataloging-in-Publication Data
Names: Jacobson, Bray, author.
Title: I do cheerleading! / Bray Jacobson.
Description: Buffalo, New York : Gareth Stevens Publishing, [2025] | Series: Learn to move! | Includes index.
Identifiers: LCCN 2023045841 | ISBN 9781482465983 (library binding) | ISBN 9781482465976 (paperback) | ISBN 9781482465990 (ebook)
Subjects: LCSH: Cheerleading–Juvenile literature. | Cheers–Juvenile literature.
Classification: LCC LB3635 .J34 2025 | DDC 791.6/4–dc23/eng/20231017
LC record available at https://lccn.loc.gov/2023045841

First Edition

Published in 2025 by
Gareth Stevens Publishing
2544 Clinton Street
Buffalo, NY 14224

Editor: Kristen Nelson
Designer: Leslie Taylor

Photo credits: Cover, p. 17 Dmytro Zinkevych/Shutterstock.com; pp. 5, 9, 15 Cherednychenko Ihor/Shutterstock.com; p. 7 Ixepop/Shutterstock.com; p. 11 FatCamera/iStockphoto.com.com; p. 13 Pressmaster/Shutterstock.com; p. 19 standret/iStockphoto.com; p. 21 Anton Vierietin/Shutterstock.com; p. 23 A_Lesik/Shutterstock.com.

Printed in the United States of America

CPSIA compliance information: Batch #CS25GS: For further information contact Gareth Stevens, New York, New York at 1-800-542-2595.

Contents

It is time to go to cheer!

My friend Claudia does cheer too.
She wears a ponytail!

I am dressed to move.
I wear a skirt.
I wear sneakers.

My friend Claudia does
cheer too.
She wears a ponytail!

We stretch first.
We touch our toes.
We reach to the side.

Miss Shannon is my
cheer coach.
She shows us some moves.

We move our arms up and down.
We turn left and right.

We learn a cheer.
We say it together!
We use our pom-poms.

It is time to tumble. Charlotte can do a cartwheel!

Bella likes jumps best.
She keeps her
arms straight.
She pulls her knees up.
This is a tuck jump!

We work as a team.
Cheer is so much fun!

Words to Know

coach

pom-pom

tuck jump

Index